MINDFULNESS
FOR DOGS

SAM HART

summersdale

MINDFULNESS FOR DOGS

Summersdale Publishers Ltd
46 West Street
Chichester
West Sussex
PO19 1RP
UK

www.summersdale.com

Printed and bound in the Czech Republic

ISBN: 978-1-84953-781-0

Substantial discounts on bulk quantities of Summersdale books are available to corporations, professional associations and other organisations. For details contact Nicky Douglas by telephone: +44 (0) 1243 756902, fax: +44 (0) 1243 786300 or email: nicky@summersdale.com.

To..

From...

ALL WE NEED TO MAKE US HAPPY IS
SOMETHING TO BE ENTHUSIASTIC ABOUT.

BEFORE BEGINNING THE DAY, TAKE
THREE DEEP BREATHS, ALLOWING
THE AIR TO OPEN UP YOUR CHEST
AND LENGTHEN YOUR SPINE.

GET OUT OF YOUR HEAD AND INTO YOUR HEART. THINK LESS, FEEL MORE.

EVERY SO OFTEN, AS YOU GO ABOUT YOUR DAY, SAY QUIETLY TO YOURSELF, 'I AM AT PEACE.'

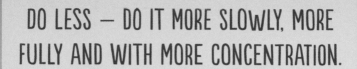

DO LESS — DO IT MORE SLOWLY, MORE FULLY AND WITH MORE CONCENTRATION.

AS YOU WAKE UP, THINK ABOUT
THE THINGS YOU CAN SMELL
BEFORE OPENING YOUR EYES.

TAKE NOTICE OF OBJECTS THAT ATTRACT YOU ON A WALK. BRING INTO SHARP FOCUS YOUR SENSES OF SIGHT, SOUND, SMELL, TOUCH AND TASTE.

IF YOU FIND YOURSELF FEELING ANXIOUS OR DWELLING ON BAD THOUGHTS, CLOSE YOUR EYES AND PICTURE YOUR FAVOURITE PLACE.

EVERY DAY IS PRECIOUS.

STOP STILL. MENTALLY SCAN YOUR
BODY FOR TENSION AND THEN RELAX.

TAKE SOME TIME TO SIMPLY BE.

DON'T WORRY ABOUT HOW FAR YOU
HAVE TO TRAVEL. FOCUS ON THE
PRESENT, KNOWING THAT WITH EVERY
STEP YOU ARE NEARING YOUR GOAL.

ALLOW YOURSELF A FEW
MINUTES TO PLAY AND HAVE FUN
BEFORE STARTING A BUSY DAY.

ACCEPT EVERYONE FOR WHO THEY ARE.

NO DAY IS SO BAD THAT IT CAN'T BE
FIXED WITH SOME GENTLE RELAXATION.

SEE FRIENDS REGULARLY — CHERISH YOUR MOMENTS TOGETHER AND LET THEM KNOW HOW SPECIAL THEY ARE.

LOOKING AT THE BEAUTY IN
THE WORLD IS THE FIRST STEP
TO OPENING YOUR MIND.

DECIDE WHAT ENERGISES YOU — IF IT'S SPENDING TIME WITH LOVED ONES, DO IT TODAY.

MAKE TODAY A 'NO RUSH' DAY. HANDLE EACH OF YOUR ACTIVITIES WITH THE ATTENTION AND CARE THEY DESERVE.

YOU CANNOT CONTROL THE RESULTS,
BUT YOU CAN CONTROL YOUR ACTIONS.

MAKE A REAL POINT OF LISTENING TO
WHAT OTHERS ARE SAYING BEFORE
OFFERING YOUR POINT OF VIEW.
LISTEN MORE AND TALK LESS.

THE LITTLE THINGS?
THE LITTLE MOMENTS?
THEY AREN'T LITTLE.

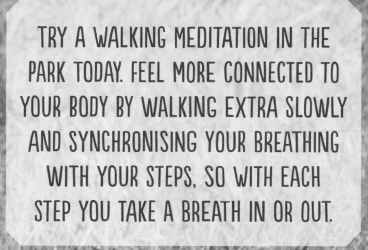

TRY A WALKING MEDITATION IN THE PARK TODAY. FEEL MORE CONNECTED TO YOUR BODY BY WALKING EXTRA SLOWLY AND SYNCHRONISING YOUR BREATHING WITH YOUR STEPS, SO WITH EACH STEP YOU TAKE A BREATH IN OR OUT.

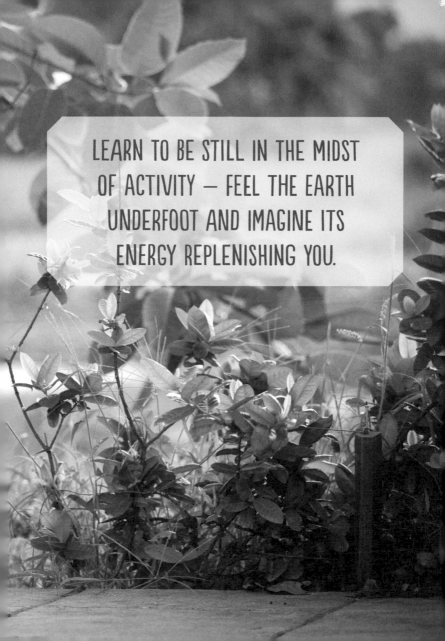

LEARN TO BE STILL IN THE MIDST OF ACTIVITY — FEEL THE EARTH UNDERFOOT AND IMAGINE ITS ENERGY REPLENISHING YOU.

REMEMBER THAT ALL LIFE IS PRECIOUS.
BE MINDFUL OF OTHERS — BOTH
LOVED ONES AND STRANGERS.

REMEMBER: THERE ARE THOUSANDS
OF REASONS TO LIVE THIS LIFE,
EVERY ONE OF THEM SUFFICIENT.

BECOME CONSCIOUS OF YOUR BREATH
AND VISUALISE IT FILLING THE WHOLE
OF YOUR BODY. A FEW MOMENTS OF
THIS AWARENESS AND YOU WILL
FEEL LIGHTER AND BRIGHTER.

FREEDOM IS INSTANTANEOUS
THE MOMENT WE ACCEPT
THINGS AS THEY ARE.

GIVE YOUR UNDIVIDED ATTENTION
TO THOSE YOU LOVE AND
REMEMBER TO SAY 'I LOVE YOU'.

CLEAR YOUR HEAD FOR A FEW MINUTES WHILE YOU FOCUS ON BEING IN THE PRESENT.

EMBRACE THE SMELLS OF A NEW ENVIRONMENT: FOCUS ON THE AROMA OF A FLOWER OR NEWLY CUT GRASS.

IF YOUR MIND STARTS TO FLAG,
HAVE A GOOD STRETCH OR
GO FOR A RUN.

LAUGH — EVERY DAY.
IT'S GOOD FOR YOU.

REPEAT THIS AFFIRMATION IN
YOUR MIND WHENEVER YOU
REMEMBER: 'SLOW DOWN'.

OPEN ALL THE WINDOWS AROUND YOU — FEEL THE BREEZE ON YOUR SKIN AND SMELL THE FRESH AIR.

WE'RE SO BUSY WATCHING OUT FOR WHAT'S JUST AHEAD OF US THAT WE DON'T TAKE TIME TO ENJOY WHERE WE ARE: LIVE IN THE PRESENT.

LOOK AT EVERYTHING AS THOUGH YOU WERE SEEING IT FOR THE FIRST TIME.

IF YOU SPEED THROUGH LIFE YOU FORGET
NOT ONLY WHERE YOU'VE BEEN, BUT
ALSO WHERE YOU'RE GOING. LIFE IS
NOT A RACE BUT A JOURNEY TO BE
SAVOURED EACH STEP OF THE WAY.

RECOGNISE THAT THOUGHTS ARE SIMPLY THOUGHTS; YOU DON'T NEED TO BELIEVE THEM OR REACT TO THEM.

WHEN YOU REACH A CALM AND QUIET MEDITATIVE STATE, THAT IS WHEN YOU CAN HEAR THE SOUND OF SILENCE.

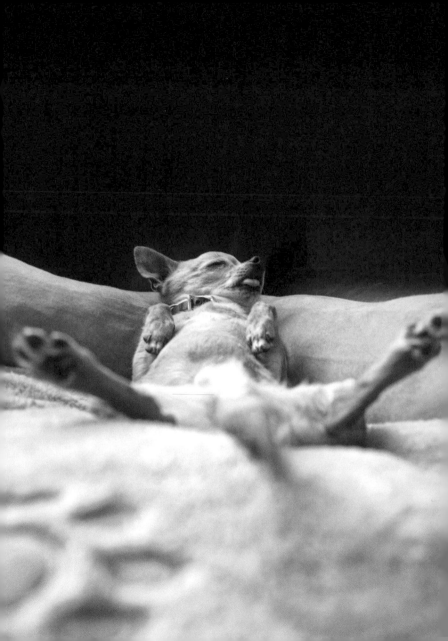

REMEMBER: YOU DON'T ALWAYS HAVE TO SAY 'YES'. OPEN UP SOME SPACE FOR QUIET IN YOUR LIFE BY SAYING 'NO'.

TODAY MAKE A CONSCIOUS EFFORT TO REDUCE YOUR TALKING AND SEE HOW SILENCE CAN HOLD YOU IN A CALM SPACE.

SPEND A SUMMER'S DAY WALKING BAREFOOT ON THE BEACH, FEELING THE WARMTH AND ENJOYING THE SOFT SAND IN BETWEEN YOUR TOES AS YOU TAKE EACH STEP.

STOP EVERY ONCE IN A WHILE
TO COUNT ALL THE BLESSINGS
IN YOUR LIFE.

THE PLACE TO BE HAPPY IS HERE;
THE TIME TO BE HAPPY IS NOW.

If you're interested in finding out more about our books, find us on Facebook at **Summersdale Publishers** and follow us on Twitter at **@Summersdale**.

www.summersdale.com